SHE RISES
S T U D I O S

THE MINDFUL JOURNEY

FINDING PEACE THROUGH *Mental Health*

HANNA OLIVAS & ADRIANA LUNA CARLOS
ALONG WITH 7 INSPIRING AUTHORS

ISBN: 978-1-960136-46-6

Table of Contents

INTRODUCTION

She Rises Studios was created and inspired by the mother-daughter duo Hanna Olivas and Adriana Luna Carlos. In the middle of 2020, when the world was at one of its most vulnerable times, we saw the need to embrace women globally by offering inspirational quotes, blogs, and articles. Then, in March of 2021, we launched our very own Women's Empowerment Podcast: *She Rises Studios Podcast*.

It is now one of the most sought out Women based podcasts both nationally and internationally. You can find us on your favorite podcast platforms, such as Spotify, Google Podcasts, Apple Podcasts, IHeartRadio, and much more! We didn't stop there. Establishing a safe space for women has become an even deeper need. Due to a global pandemic, women lost their businesses, employment, homes, finances, spouses, and more.

We decided to form the She Rises Studios Community Facebook Group. An environment strictly for women about women. Our focus in this group is to educate and celebrate women globally. To meet them exactly where they are on their journey.

It's a group of Ordinary Women Doing EXTRAordinary Things.

As our network continued to expand, it became apparent that there was a pressing need to guide and empower women grappling with insecurities, uncertainties, fears, and more. It was from this realization that **"The Mindful Journey"** anthology was born.

The Mindful Journey | Finding Peace Through Mental Health

In our relentless, fast-paced world, where life's demands often feel overwhelming, the quest for inner peace and mental balance has become an urgent necessity. **The Mindful Journey: Finding Peace**

Through Mental Health is your steadfast companion on this profound voyage of self-discovery and healing.

Within these pages, you'll embark on an extraordinary exploration of the human mind, guided by the collective wisdom of those who've faced their mental health struggles. This book isn't merely a guide; it's a holistic roadmap to wellness, woven with insight, inspiration, and hope.

Our journey begins with the understanding that mental health is a unique, personal journey. Just as no two wilderness paths are identical, no two minds are alike. **The Mindful Journey** recognizes the distinct challenges and experiences each individual brings to their quest for peace. Within these pages, you'll find a treasure trove of knowledge and stories, a toolkit to navigate the intricate labyrinth of mental health.

This anthology is a testament to the power of shared human experiences. Alongside expert advice, you'll find personal stories and anecdotes from those who've stood precisely where you may find yourself today. These narratives aren't mere accounts of struggle; they're tales of resilience, triumph, and healing. They serve as beacons of hope, reminding us that even in the darkest of nights, there's a dawn awaiting its moment to break.

As you delve into these stories and absorb the guidance within these pages, you'll discover a profound sense of community, a reminder that on your journey to inner peace, you are not alone. These anecdotes, shared with candor and vulnerability, will light your path and reveal the countless possibilities that lie ahead.

The Mindful Journey is more than a collection of words; it's an invitation to embrace mindfulness, compassion, and self-discovery as tools to shape your destiny. It pays homage to the indomitable resilience of the human spirit and the boundless strength within each one of us.

Whether you seek solace for yourself in the turbulence of your own thoughts or strive to support someone you hold dear, this book provides the knowledge, resources, and inspiration necessary for a truly transformative journey.

The Mindful Journey is your gateway to the cultivation of peace, the embrace of joy, and the fortification of resilience. It is your compass on the intricate path toward mental wellness. With its engaging and accessible style, this book stands as an indispensable companion for anyone embarking on the voyage to discover peace through mental health. So, dear reader, commence your transformative journey with an open heart and an open mind. Your mindful journey begins now.

She Rises Studios offers:

- She Rises Studios Publishing
- She Rises Studios Public Relations
- She Rises Studios Podcast (FREE to Listen to!)
- She Rises Studios Magazine
- Rise with Hanna Olivas - Featured on FENIX TV
- She Rises Studios Community Facebook Page (FREE to Join!)
- She Rises Studios Academy
- KNOWN SRS
- FENIX TV

We won't stop encouraging women to be Unstoppable. This is just the beginning of our global movement.

She Rises, She Leads, She Lives...

With Love,
HANNA OLIVAS
ADRIANA LUNA CARLOS
SHE RISES STUDIOS
www.sherisesstudios.com

Hanna Olivas

Founder & CEO of She Rises Studios
Podcast & TV Host | Best Selling Author | Influential Speaker |
Blood Cancer Advocate | #BAUW Movement Creator

https://www.linkedin.com/company/she-rises-studios/
https://www.instagram.com/sherisesstudios_llc/
https://www.facebook.com/sherisesstudios
www.SheRisesStudios.com

Author, Speaker, and Founder. Hanna was born and raised in Las Vegas, Nevada, and has paved her way to becoming one of the most influential women of 2022. Hanna is the co-founder of She Rises Studios and the founder of the Brave & Beautiful Blood Cancer Foundation. Her journey started in 2017 when she was first diagnosed with Multiple Myeloma, an incurable blood cancer. Now more than ever, her focus is to empower other women to become leaders because The Future is Female. She is currently traveling and speaking publicly to women to educate them on entrepreneurship, leadership, and owning the female power within.

THE MINDFUL JOURNEY - A PATH TO PERSONAL GROWTH

By Hanna Olivas

I've always been mindful of everything, from how I think to how my body feels, and even mindful of others and things around me. I'm especially mindful of my thoughts, whether they are good or bad. I watch and listen to everyone who is within my close proximity. I pay attention to detail, body language, and action. I think, in some ways, this is both a blessing and a curse. One of the most pivotal moments in my mindful journey began at a young age when I was exposed to a challenging childhood, which followed me for many, many years.

Being mindful of your journey is vital. You must pay close attention to your life's details. If you don't, you will wake up one day and wonder where the time has gone. What have I done on my journey? These are questions that you may ponder as you embark on your own mindful journey.

The Essence of Mindfulness

Mindfulness is not just a trendy concept; it's a way of life that can bring profound changes to your overall well-being. It's about being fully present in the moment, conscious of your thoughts and actions, and aware of the world around you. This practice extends to various aspects of life, touching on your health, wealth, life, business, finance, relationships, children, spouse or partner, and yourself. Being mindful in these areas can help you lead a more fulfilling and purposeful life.

Health and Mindfulness

Your health is the foundation of a fulfilling life. To be mindful of your health, you must pay attention to your body and its signals. Regular exercise, a balanced diet, and adequate rest are crucial. Additionally, practicing mindful eating can help you make healthier food choices, enjoy your meals more, and avoid overeating.

Mindfulness can also enhance your mental health. By acknowledging your thoughts and emotions without judgment, you can better manage stress and anxiety. Mindful meditation and deep breathing exercises can be powerful tools for promoting mental well-being.

Wealth and Mindfulness

Mindfulness in wealth involves a conscious awareness of your financial decisions. Being mindful of your spending habits, savings, and investments can lead to a more secure financial future. Consider your long-term financial goals and how your current actions align with them. This can help you make more informed financial choices.

Life and Mindfulness

Every moment of your life is precious. Being mindful of life means savoring these moments and not taking them for granted. Whether it's watching a sunset, spending time with loved ones, or pursuing a passion, embracing life's experiences with mindfulness can bring a deeper sense of contentment.

Business and Mindfulness

In the business world, mindfulness can enhance your performance and decision-making. Being fully engaged in tasks, listening actively to colleagues, and approaching challenges with a clear mind can lead to more effective outcomes. Mindfulness can also reduce workplace stress and improve overall job satisfaction.

Finance and Mindfulness

Being mindful of your finances extends beyond budgeting. It involves understanding your financial goals, recognizing the value of money, and making responsible choices regarding your spending and investments. Mindful financial management can lead to financial security and peace of mind.

Relationships and Mindfulness

Mindful relationships are built on communication, empathy, and understanding. Being present when you interact with loved ones can strengthen your connections. Listen actively, express yourself honestly, and show appreciation for the people who enrich your life.

Mindfulness can deeply impact your role as a parent and partner. Being present with your children, understanding their needs, and fostering a loving and nurturing environment can help them thrive. In your romantic relationship, mindfulness can lead to better communication and a stronger bond.

Furthermore, mindfulness towards yourself is crucial. This self-awareness allows you to recognize your own needs, desires, and limitations. It enables self-compassion and self-improvement, leading to personal growth and inner peace.

Sharing Mindfulness

Helping others reach a state of mindfulness can be a fulfilling endeavor. By being an example of mindfulness in your own life, you can inspire those around you. Encourage open conversations about mindfulness and share your experiences. You can also introduce mindfulness practices such as meditation or yoga to friends and family, helping them to start their own journeys.

The Importance of Mindfulness

Mindfulness is essential because it brings you into the present moment, allowing you to fully experience life. It reduces stress, promotes emotional well-being, and strengthens your relationships. Mindfulness can lead to better decision-making, increased productivity, and overall life satisfaction. Moreover, it helps you make conscious choices that align with your values and goals.

In a world where distractions and fast-paced living are the norm, mindfulness offers a way to reconnect with yourself and those around you. It's a path to personal growth, self-awareness, and a more fulfilling life. Embrace your mindful journey, and encourage others to do the same. Your mindful choices today can shape a brighter, more intentional future.

Strategies for Enhancing Mindfulness

Health

Mindful Eating: Pay close attention to what you eat, how you eat, and why you eat. Savor each bite, eat slowly, and listen to your body's hunger and fullness cues. This can help you make healthier food choices and prevent overeating.

Exercise Mindfully: When you engage in physical activities, focus on the sensations in your body. Tune in to your breath, the movement of your muscles, and the environment around you. This enhances the benefits of exercise and helps reduce stress.

Meditation and Deep Breathing: Incorporate meditation and deep breathing exercises into your daily routine. This can calm your mind, reduce stress, and improve your mental and emotional well-being.

Wealth

Financial Awareness: Keep track of your income and expenses. Create a budget that aligns with your financial goals and regularly review your financial status. Mindful spending and saving can lead to a more stable financial future.

Delayed Gratification: Practice delaying instant gratification for long-term financial benefits. Consider the long-term impact of your spending decisions and how they affect your financial goals.

Life

Gratitude Practice: Cultivate gratitude by regularly reflecting on the things you're thankful for. This can shift your focus from what's lacking to what you have, leading to increased happiness and contentment.

Mindful Experiences: Fully engage in activities you enjoy. Put away distractions like smartphones and immerse yourself in the moment, whether it's hiking, reading, or spending quality time with loved ones.

Business

Active Listening: In the workplace, practice active listening. Pay full attention to your colleagues or clients during conversations. This fosters better understanding and rapport.

Stress Reduction: Use mindfulness techniques to manage workplace stress. Take short breaks for deep breathing, practice mindfulness meditation, or create a calming workspace to boost productivity and reduce anxiety.

Finance

Financial Planning: Create a financial plan that aligns with your long-term goals. Regularly review your financial progress and adjust your plan as needed. This can help you make informed financial decisions.

Mindful Spending: Before making a purchase, pause and ask yourself whether it aligns with your financial goals. Mindful spending can prevent impulse buying and promote responsible financial behavior.

Relationships

Empathy: Practice empathy in your relationships. Put yourself in the other person's shoes, actively listen to their concerns, and respond with understanding and compassion.

Effective Communication: Improve your communication skills by being mindful of your words and tone. Use "I" statements to express your feelings and avoid blame or criticism.

Children, Spouse, and Self

Quality Time: Spend quality time with your children and partner. Put away distractions, be present, and engage in activities that foster bonding and communication.

Self-Reflection: Regularly engage in self-reflection to understand your own needs, values, and goals. This self-awareness can guide your personal growth journey.

Encouraging Mindfulness in Others

Lead by Example: Your own mindful practices can inspire others. When people see the positive impact mindfulness has on your life, they may be more inclined to explore it themselves.

Open Dialogue: Encourage open and honest conversations about mindfulness with friends and family. Share your experiences and listen to theirs. Offer support and resources to help them get started.

Mindfulness Workshops or Classes: Consider organizing or attending mindfulness workshops, classes, or retreats with others. These can provide a structured introduction to mindfulness practices.

The Profound Importance of Mindfulness

The significance of mindfulness lies in its power to transform your life. It can lead to increased awareness, improved mental and emotional health, healthier relationships, financial stability, and personal growth. By living mindfully and sharing this philosophy with others, you not only enhance your own life but contribute to a more mindful and compassionate world.

In your journey towards mindfulness, remember that it's not about achieving perfection but rather progress. Small, consistent steps can lead to profound changes. Embrace mindfulness in every aspect of your life, and watch as it unfolds into a journey of self-discovery and fulfillment.

The Benefits of Mindfulness

As I continued my journey into mindfulness, I began to experience the many benefits it offers. These benefits were not just limited to my personal life but extended to my professional and social life as well.

One of the most striking benefits was the reduction of stress. In a fast-paced world, stress can take a toll on our mental and physical health. But through mindfulness practices like meditation and deep breathing, I found a way to manage and reduce stress. Whenever I felt overwhelmed or anxious, I would take a few minutes to meditate, focusing on my breath and letting go of the tension. Over time, I noticed that I became more resilient in the face of challenges, and stress had less of an impact on me.

Another significant benefit was an improved sense of focus and productivity. Mindfulness helped me stay present in the moment, which in turn increased my ability to concentrate on tasks. Whether it was working on a project, reading a book, or having a conversation, I was able to give my full attention to the task at hand. This heightened focus not only improved the quality of my work but also allowed me to accomplish more in less time.

Mindfulness also had a profound impact on my relationships. By being fully present with loved ones, I was able to listen more attentively and connect on a deeper level. My empathy and understanding grew, making me a better friend, partner, and parent. When conflicts arose, I found that approaching them with a calm and clear mind, rather than reacting impulsively, led to more constructive and harmonious resolutions.

In my professional life, the benefits of mindfulness became even more evident. Active listening and clear-headed decision-making were essential in the workplace. By practicing mindfulness, I improved my ability to understand my colleagues and clients, leading to better working relationships and more successful collaborations. Additionally, my stress management techniques allowed me to maintain a sense of composure during high-pressure situations, enhancing my performance and job satisfaction.

The Journey of Personal Growth

As I continued down the path of mindfulness, I realized that it was not just a set of practices but a journey of personal growth. It was about understanding myself on a deeper level, recognizing my own needs, desires, and limitations, and ultimately, striving to become the best version of myself.

This journey required self-reflection, a process that allowed me to delve into the depths of my thoughts and emotions. It was not always easy, as self-reflection often meant confronting aspects of myself that I had long ignored or denied. However, it was through this introspection that I began to make positive changes in my life. I addressed unhealthy habits, faced past traumas, and worked towards a greater sense of self-acceptance.

Self-compassion became a fundamental aspect of my personal growth. I learned to treat myself with the same kindness and understanding that I extended to others. Instead of being overly critical of my own mistakes and imperfections, I adopted a more forgiving attitude. This self-compassion not only alleviated the burden of self-judgment but also motivated me to improve and grow.

Personal growth was not limited to my inner world; it also extended to my interactions with others. I realized the power of setting healthy boundaries and communicating my needs effectively. It was not about being selfish, but about ensuring that my relationships were based on mutual respect and understanding. As I grew and changed, I found that some relationships evolved and strengthened, while others naturally drifted away.

Embracing mindfulness in every aspect of my life allowed me to align my choices with my values and goals. I no longer lived on autopilot, but made conscious decisions that reflected my true aspirations. This was particularly evident in my financial decisions, where mindful spending and long-term financial planning ensured that my money was used to support my dreams and well-being.

Sharing the Gift of Mindfulness

As my own journey of mindfulness continued, I felt a deep desire to share the gift I had received with others. I realized that by being an example of mindfulness in my own life, I could inspire those around me to embark on their journeys.

One way I encouraged mindfulness in others was through open and honest conversations. I would often engage friends and family in discussions about the benefits of mindfulness and my own experiences. By sharing my journey, I hoped to inspire them to explore mindfulness themselves. Sometimes, these conversations led to a ripple effect, as they in turn introduced mindfulness practices into their lives.

For those who were interested in a more structured approach, I encouraged participation in mindfulness workshops or classes. These settings provided a supportive environment for learning and practicing mindfulness techniques. It allowed individuals to explore mindfulness in a group, share their experiences, and receive guidance from experienced instructors.

By leading by example, openly discussing mindfulness, and introducing structured opportunities for exploration, I hoped to make mindfulness more accessible to those around me. I firmly believed that the benefits of mindfulness were not to be kept a secret but shared with anyone seeking a more fulfilling and purposeful life.

The Ongoing Journey

In the world of mindfulness, the journey is never truly complete. It's not about reaching a destination but about embracing a continuous process of growth and self-discovery. As I reflected on my own path, I realized that mindfulness was not about achieving perfection but about making progress.

Small, consistent steps led to profound changes in my life. Each day was an opportunity to be more present, to be kinder to myself and others, and to make choices that aligned with my values and goals. The journey of mindfulness was a daily commitment to living life to the fullest and encouraging those around me to do the same.

In closing, I invite you to embark on your own mindful journey. Take those first steps towards greater self-awareness, well-being, and personal growth. Embrace mindfulness in all aspects of your life, and watch as it unfolds into a remarkable journey of transformation and fulfillment. Remember, it's not about where you start; it's about the direction in which you choose to move.

Adriana Luna Carlos

Founder and CEO of She Rises Studios & FENIX TV

https://www.linkedin.com/in/adriana-luna-carlos/
https://www.facebook.com/adrianalunacarlos
https://www.instagram.com/sherisesstudios_llc/
https://www.sherisesstudios.com/
https://www.srslatina.com/
https://fenixtv.app/

Adriana Luna Carlos is an accomplished web and graphic designer, author, and mentor with a passion for helping women succeed in life and business. With over 10 years of experience in graphic and web arts, Adriana has built a reputation as an innovative leader and entrepreneur. In 2020, she co-founded She Rises Studios, a multi-digital media company and publishing house that has helped countless clients achieve their branding and marketing goals. In 2023, she co-created FENIX TV, an online streaming platform that showcases stories of people breaking barriers, shattering stereotypes, and triumphing against the odds.

As an advocate for women's success, Adriana challenges her clients and mentees to strive for nothing less than excellence. She has a deep understanding of the insecurities and challenges that women often face in the business world and provides the guidance and resources needed to overcome them. Her success as a business leader and entrepreneur has made her a sought-after mentor and speaker at events around the world.

Through her work, Adriana has demonstrated a commitment to creating opportunities for women to succeed in business and life. Her passion for innovation, leadership, and women's empowerment has made her a respected figure in the business community, and her impact will undoubtedly continue to inspire and empower women for years to come.

PERCEPTIONS AND REFLECTIONS: THE MIRROR OF SELF-WORTH

By Adriana Luna Carlos

Life's thrown its fair share of curveballs at me. Each one, a lesson, wrapped up in the guise of hardships and challenges. It's easy to lose yourself, to get caught up in what the world thinks of you, letting their perceptions shape your reflection. But here's what I've learned: life's too short to let someone else's opinion dictate your worth.

I used to get bogged down by people's judgments. It was like carrying an invisible weight that subtly, yet profoundly, influenced my steps. But along the way, something shifted. I realized that people's opinions were more like mirrors reflecting their own thoughts and insecurities. Their words, their labels, they weren't really about me; they were echoes of their own inner dialogue.

Dealing with life's obstacles, I discovered a lot about my resilience and strength. Every difficulty, every nook and corner of hardship I found myself in, became a place where I grew, adapted, and learned something valuable. It became clear that these weren't just roadblocks but stepping stones, guiding me toward a more resilient version of myself.

Recognizing my own worth became a game-changer. It became my compass, helping me navigate through life's ups and downs with a sense of purpose and confidence. No longer was my worth up for negotiation—it became a solid foundation on which I built my decisions, actions, and relationships.

There have been countless moments in my life marked by the harsh trials of adversity, each one molding me into a stronger individual. From the seemingly trivial, like enduring teasing for being the "little white girl" in a predominantly Hispanic family, to the profoundly traumatic experiences, such as surviving a decade of molestation by a family member. These ordeals, and many more in between, have been arduous journeys through pain and struggle. However, each challenge, in its unique way, contributed to my resilience, forging me into the individual I am today, capable of withstanding adversity with a reinforced spirit and unyielding strength.

In embracing my worth, life began to reflect back the strength, courage, and determination I felt inside. The journey wasn't always smooth sailing; there were bumps, twists, and turns. But it led to a transformation that allowed me to thrive, flourish, and move forward with authenticity and a deeper understanding of who I truly am.

For those of you reading this and struggling with your identity, feeling cornered by the perceptions of others, I'd say: Dive deep within. Your self-worth is a treasure waiting to be discovered. Here are some steps you can take:

- **Journaling:** Start by documenting your feelings. Writing can be therapeutic, helping you navigate and understand your emotions better.
- **Find Your Outlet:** It could be music, art, sports, or any other form. Engage in activities that allow you to express and connect with yourself.
- **Seek Support:** Talk to someone you trust. Sharing your feelings can provide clarity and perspective.
- **Challenge Negative Thoughts:** Every time a negative thought about yourself arises, challenge it. Ask yourself if it's genuinely how you feel or if it's an external perception influencing you.
- **Celebrate Small Wins:** Recognize and celebrate every small achievement. These will act as stepping stones towards building your self-worth.

Here's a little heart-to-heart on how life tends to unfold. We all start with dreams in our eyes and a spring in our step, ready to take on the world. But then, life, being the unpredictable journey it is, throws us some curveballs. These unexpected turns can shake us, make us stumble, sometimes even bring us to our knees. But guess what? They also give us the strength we didn't know we had, teach us lessons that become life's treasures, and mold us into better versions of ourselves.

So, how do we navigate these tricky turns? How do we ensure that we don't just survive but thrive amidst adversities? Here's a heartfelt guide with some practical tips to help you sail through, to maintain a positive mindset, and to uncover the silver linings in the clouds that life brings along.

1. The Starting Point: Enthusiasm and Anticipation

- In the beginning, there's excitement, dreams are bright, and the path ahead seems clear and straightforward.

2. Encounter with Curveballs: Reality Check

- Life throws challenges, unexpected twists, and turns, forcing a recalibration of the journey.

3. The Battle: Resilience and Perseverance

- A phase of struggle, fighting through difficulties, a test of determination and resilience.

4. Emerging Stronger: Lessons Learned

- Overcoming hurdles, learning lessons, adapting, and acquiring new strengths.

5. Continuous Growth: Nurturing the Mindset

- Ongoing development, maintaining a healthy mindset, and preparing for future challenges.

Strategies for Navigating Life's Labyrinth

1. Embrace the Unexpected

   - Accept that life is unpredictable. Use challenges as opportunities to learn and grow.

2. Cultivate Resilience

   - Develop a strong mental fortitude. Practice bouncing back from adversities with a positive mindset.

3. Engage in Self-Care and Reflection

   - Prioritize self-care routines. Regularly take time to reflect, understand, and process your thoughts and emotions.

4. Connect and Communicate

   - Build a support system. Share and discuss your feelings and experiences with trusted individuals.

5. Continuous Learning and Adaptation

   - Stay open to new learning experiences. Adapt and adjust your strategies and approaches as you navigate through life.

6. Practice Mindfulness and Gratitude

   - Engage in mindfulness practices. Cultivate a habit of acknowledging and being grateful for the positive aspects of life.

7. Set Realistic Goals and Celebrate Achievements

   - Set attainable goals for your journey. Celebrate the small and significant achievements along the way.

Reflection Points to Consider During the Journey

- What are the curveballs that life has thrown at me, and how have they shaped my journey?
- Which battles have tested my resilience the most, and what strategies helped me to overcome them?
- How can I continuously nurture my mindset to maintain a healthy perspective on life's challenges?

In the end, it's all about perception and reflection. The way we perceive ourselves plays a crucial role in our journey of self-discovery. By reflecting on our experiences and learning from them, we can pave the way to a stronger sense of self-worth and identity. So, whenever you feel lost amidst the chaos of external perceptions, remember to turn inward. Your inner self holds the answers.

Ashley Zuidema

Educator/Author

https://www.linkedin.com/in/ashley-zuidema-5388b538
https://www.facebook.com/ashley.kammeraadzuidema
https://www.instagram.com/ashleyzuidema/

Mother and Wife, Life-long Learner, Educator, and Author. Ashley was born and raised in Holland, MI. Over the last 15 years, she has utilized her passion for education and learning while obtaining two Master's degrees. One from Baker College in Business, and the other from Grand Valley State University in Education. Ashley enjoys reading, crafting/journal making, and her love for her animals. She is determined to be successful at whatever she does and takes pride in her hardworking nature.

Ashley is currently working as an Instructional Assistant at a local elementary school. She has attempted to take the Michigan Teachers Certification Test multiple times and finds that she enjoys the ability to write and the added freedom much more enjoyable. Ashley's mission is to help other women who have been in abusive relationships to show they can do so much more if given the chance.

CRAWLING OUT OF THE DARKNESS

By Ashley Zuidema

"Happiness can be found even in the darkest of times, when one only remembers to turn on the light."
—Albus Dumbledore

I think Albus Dumbledore said it the best: true happiness really depends on when we are in our darkest moments. Only in the darkness of depression do we really need to push ourselves to find our own light. Depression in the darkest moments can sometimes feel like you are way down the rabbit hole and trying to find a light switch, reaching for the sun. Symptoms of depression create a feeling of being on a sandy hill, and no matter how hard you try to climb you are still slipping further and further down. Even if you dig your feet in, there is still momentum that is lost when grabbing at the sand.

Why is it we say we are depressed? How long does depression really last? It gets harder and harder to answer these questions when life continues to throw us curve balls. Some days it feels like we wake up, but are too tired to actually stay awake. It almost feels like staying in bed is a much better option. Some days this is what the body needs and that is ok. During my journey there were many times I stayed in bed, lay on the couch all day, and just plain forgot about life. If you are finding that you are making a habit of it, it might be time to get up and push yourself to do something you enjoy doing.

Depression is a form of mental disorder and is very real. For some individuals, it is worse than others, while some are able to quickly adapt and move forward. Mental health in any form is a difficult topic to openly discuss for anyone. There are many forms of mental illness that some people suffer from. The hardest part is to distinguish your symptoms from any other form.

The focus of this chapter is to discuss depression, the impact it has had on me, and how I was able to turn on the light a little easier. Although this chapter is not going to detail all the events in my life, I do plan to share a few moments and how I was able to pull through it. The suggestions that are presented in this chapter are what helped me.

Jumping directly to medication is not always the best resolution. The medication can sometimes have the opposite effect. The side effects of these medications could potentially cause even more problems. Getting off of these medications can be even worse. They become a static part of your life. Currently, I am on a form of medication that I have been on for years. I worry that one day, I will not be able to get away from them. Only time will tell.

What do you think about when considering what is causing your depression? What is it that you reflect on daily? Considering the "what ifs" in life never helps, as it is looking back instead of forward. Trying to consider what would have been, what "would it have been like if…" and thinking "I wonder what it would have been like if I wouldn't have done that." The only thing we can consider now is how are we going to make a change. How can we find a way to build ourselves up and move forward? When feeling down, we need to ask ourselves these questions.

As I grow into adulthood, it gets harder and harder to remember what my childhood was like. Being a willful child, I am pretty sure that I made things more difficult for myself than necessary. As a tween, my parents moved us to another city. I had lost all of my friends from school and my ability to see them quickly. This is not something a ten-year-old likes to endure. I became a rebellious child. I got pregnant at fifteen and had my firstborn at sixteen. The idea of their youngest daughter having a child did not sit well with my family. When he was born, I needed to grow up really fast. I was very thankful to my mother and sister for helping me with the baby and taking care of him while I had to work.

Being the youngest child in my family, my willfulness kicked in even more. The need for attention grew. The only attention I felt as though I received was always negative. There was abuse in the family right around this time as well. I remember events that will haunt me for the rest of my life. Don't get me wrong, there were also good times as well. Yet, with being willful, my choices also got me into trouble. Growing up, I remember there were many times that my sister and I were left with another family member or friend. My parents always seemed to travel and we ended up with someone else. In the end, I believe this opened a different level of childhood issues - abandonment became another factor in my mental health issues. I am sure my parents were trying to enjoy life, as we all do. However, when you are already struggling with abuse, it can be difficult to manage.

I never really thought being sad could mean it was depression. When I was growing up, mental health did not seem to be something anyone talked about. Depression was not even a factor at the time. The biggest challenge that I have faced since I was a child was abuse. This was at every level a person could endure. It made me hate being around this person and having to deal with them. I would do everything I could not to be at home. I went out with my friends a lot. One of my closest friends was always there when something happened. It was nice to have that support system in place.

When I was twenty-one, my mother passed away. At this point, my depression had already started and I was dealing with the concept of loss. What is it like to lose someone and be able to move past it? Most people know that grief comes in stages. This did not happen for me it has been bottled up all my life. Once you cry for so many loved ones, crying just seems to be a distant pastime. At the time of the burial of both my parents is the last time I remember crying.

My mother spoiled my sister and me. We never had to want for anything. Even though she was always working or going away, she would find some way to make it up to us. Thinking about it now, I wonder if she was trying to buy our forgiveness. Symptoms of abandonment progressed when my mother passed away from Cancer. I had lived at home with my two boys (on and off). I would never have imagined that one day I would not have a home or mother to go back to. Afterward, my father kicked me out of the house. Even before this event, I had never gotten along with my father, and the situation continued to make me feel more alone. At this point both my parents were gone and I really began to feel like an orphan.

My problem with depression and abandonment moved along even more after my best friend died in a motorcycle accident. I had just lost my mother, and then losing him felt like the whole world came crashing down and I did not know what to do with myself. I am very thankful for the boyfriend I had at the time, who was willing to help me get through it. When I couldn't get myself out of bed or manage to fix myself something to eat, he took care of me and my boys. I felt ashamed because of this. However, suffering loss after loss is not easy on one's soul.

The list of losses just kept growing from there. Over the years I have lost many family members, friends, and close relatives. Even now, so many years later, it is hard to believe they are gone. I often wonder what my mother would have thought about what I have done with my life. I can only hope that one day I will know for sure that she is proud of me. I never felt like we had made amends before she died. As most mother-daughter relationships go, our relationship was rocky as I went into my teenage years. Even though my mother worked two jobs and was consistently gone, she still was the best.

There have been many times that I have been advised to go see a therapist. I tried; it didn't help. When they tell me that I need to journal things, write letters, talk to family members, etc. I just don't see a point in it. You sit there and talk about your feelings, thoughts, and emotions. This is everything I can do with my art(s). Expressing myself through art has given me the chance to open up many ways of healing. The therapist told me to journal things, so I started to create journals. Writing letters has always been my strong suit. Additionally, sitting with one of my favorite aunts during this creative process has given me the chance to open up and talk from time to time about my past, present, and future with someone. I discovered that I do not have to be silent and hold everything in.

After reading all of this you are probably questioning why you should care. Let me ask you this; what inspires you? Inspiration can come in many forms. Much like my mother, I am always behind the camera (I am not a fan of my picture being taken) and I find so much beauty in nature. It is amazing what nature has to offer everywhere; there is so much you can do with nature. You can draw, take pictures of it, create paintings, or just sit out and appreciate it. Much of what my mother did in her life has also inspired me. I know that she worked really hard to take care of us kids. There has not been a time where I have worked at least two jobs in order to provide for my boys.

My experience with improving my depression; comes down to the following three suggestions. I found that utilizing these three steps can truly help improve your mood, put a smile on your face, and ease depression symptoms. I know these will not always apply to everyone, but they are a good start to finding that one particular escape.

1. Start by finding the one thing you really enjoy.

I have always been a "crafter" of sorts. I really enjoy creating scrapbooks. When my children were little, this was a great way to find joy in reliving these memories. I have recently begun working on crafting and creating journals and junk journals. There is so much you can do with these and the process is never-ending. This allows me time to relax, clear my mind, and find my inner creative outlet. It is even better when something you create goes exactly the way you intended it to. There is no greater feeling than that satisfaction. I enjoy finding my creative niche and using it as a means of taking my mind off things. I also learned that through crafting you are able to express yourself while showing your true feelings.

2. Be Inspired

Growing up we always had a reason to be outside. Whether it was to hang out with friends, mess around in the yard, or be out by the pool. There was rarely any time that I would be home and not be outside. Finding inspiration and peace in nature is an excellent way to battle the effects of depression. Taking a nature walk, being out by the water and/or at the beach, taking in the scenery, and admiring the views; can be very relaxing. If you like to take pictures on your phone and/or tablet, this is a great way to explore your interests and get inspired. Nature has so many different ways of showing us beauty, we just need to go look for it. Some people also use their nature adventures to meditate.

3. Distractions

As a child my favorite distraction was playing Mario Brothers on my Nintendo System. There was something about immersing myself in the game, strategic thinking, and problem-solving that appealed to me. I had to focus on the game versus what was happening in my own world. As I got older I found comfort in spending time with my friends. I had a few that I considered very close friends. Almost every day after school one or two of my friends would be at my house. This helped me greatly in finding a way to overcome difficult situations (which in my house happened often) and be able to feel ok. As time moves forward and life keeps throwing curve balls, I tend to delve into reading. There is something about getting lost in the characters' stories, picturing the scenery, feeling as though I am right there with the character, and trying to gain an understanding of what they are doing and learning about them through character development. Some may think that utilizing a distraction is never the way to go. In the end, yes the problems are always going to be there in the end. However, even if I get an hour or more of relief helps make my day that much better.

The main focus of this chapter is to focus on depression and the effects it has on us. It shows us who we really are and what we feel like we can not do. The hardest part in getting over depression; is ensuring that we utilize our skills and abilities to good use. Now, do not say you do not have the necessary skills. That would be an inaccurate statement; everyone possesses that one ability that we use for the greater good.

In the end, I learned that there is so much more to me and what I am capable of. I understand that not everything can be controlled. We need to let go and see how things pan out for us. Considering what I have been through and learned along the way, I would have never imagined that I would be sitting here writing this chapter. I am so grateful for the chance to empower other women in the fight against depression. You are beautiful in every way and are capable of anything you set your mind to. Thank you for being a part of my adventure and reading my story.

Aleena Slater

The Imperfect Teacher Au
Author & Teacher

www.linkedin.com/in/aleena-slater-44bb5913b
https://www.facebook.com/aleena.slater/
https://www.instagram.com/aslat49/

Aleena Slater is a passionate, practicing Australian Teacher, Conference Presenter, Author, and Teacher Wellbeing Advocate who has a genuine interest in supporting fellow educators to survive life and enjoy their work with children. Aleena has completed a Diploma of Community Services (Children's Services), a Bachelor of Education (Early Childhood), and a Master of Education (International). In 2017, she presented at an International Education Symposium in Darwin, N.T. about Self-regulation Impacts on Primary School Children. In 2021, she presented a Self-regulation and Mindfulness Workshop at a State Early Childhood Conference held in Brisbane. In 2022, she published her first book entitled, "How to Become a Perfect, Imperfect Teacher: Growing your Self-compassion". In 2023, she released her second book, "How to Become an Imperfect Teacher 2: Nurturing Your Own Value". Currently, she is teaching a class whilst undertaking a research project aimed at improving transition to school processes for the children in her disadvantaged community.

REGULATING AND MANAGING YOUR HEART, MIND, BODY, AND SOUL THROUGH CRISIS

By Aleena Slater

Everybody goes through intense difficulty, instability, and danger during their lifetime, but the question is, how does one survive through it to continue on? To put it another way, how does one maintain their health, well-being, family, career, fun, and friendships during a crisis? Sadly, there are no easy, definitive solutions or cheat sheets designed for people to conquer these challenges, as everyone experiences a crisis differently and with varying intensity. The timing of the crisis can also impact the intensity of a crisis at that age; responsibilities, health, beliefs, and prior experiences can all contribute to how the crisis is experienced and managed. Think of a family like a ship. It has a captain, or two, and various crew members that work together to make the vessel work. While the vessel may stop running smoothly at times, it just needs some maintenance or repairs to make it run well again. If left to deteriorate, without a captain, the ship falls apart and goes nowhere. However; people can choose to strengthen and develop themselves physically, mentally, and spiritually so that when it is their turn to steer their broken ship through rough, murky seas, they can be that captain and prepare their crew for the onslaught ahead.

To begin work on your "self", one needs to first accept that no crisis can ever really be avoided. When you think about it, it is quite plausible that every person on the planet will have poor health at some stage, lose people that they love, hurt themselves or others, receive devastating news, miss out on promotions, break up with a partner, make mistakes or let people down during their lives. So, people need to get comfortable with being uncomfortable so that when the time comes, they have the ability to view their situation through a more proactive lens. If a person cannot be proactive during a crisis, then it is likely that they will be negative and irrational, which could bring more challenges and struggles. People need to have a plan built into their minds for when things go wrong. The "plan", even though people cannot really plan for a crisis, should be centered on problem-solving and how to "fix" something, or anything, to decrease the struggle or better still, break free of it. This plan need not be comprehensive at all, rather it should contain a handful of practical, adaptable, and sustainable strategies that can be recalled quickly and will form part of the reprieve or solution to the crisis in the long run.

People seem to have plans and strategies for when events happen that affect finances. They plan ahead of obvious potential crises such as having life insurance, car insurance, home insurance, and health insurance for instance, where paying into these funds can support people in managing financial or grief challenges during or after a crisis. This is similar to having a will or trust account for children or family members who will benefit after a death or when they come of age. It is terrible to think that people generally only consider the financial, ownership or property impacts that a crisis can bring rather than the sometimes irreparable damage it can have on their health, mind, family structures, and relationships. Life is short, and humans come into the world without money or possessions, and they will exit the world in the exact same way. Hence, there needs to be greater emphasis placed on how strong and healthy the mind needs to be during a crisis in order to get through it with minimal long-term impact. A person's life, the people in it, their health, love, happiness, progress, success, relationships, passions, hopes, and dreams will always be what one is remembered for. With this in mind, nurturing and strengthening the mind and developing mindfulness as a means of navigating one's ship through complex situations or events is an absolute priority.

Unexpected and unfavorable events leave most people in shock as brains and bodies sense some danger, detect threats, and begin the work to fight the challenge or avoid it. Fighting the challenge often leads to exhaustion and burnout, and avoiding it only allows it to fester more and seep into all areas of life. Add the challenge to a busy family, demanding career, personal health, and relationship goals, and suddenly it turns into several challenges that soon spiral out of control. The key to really surviving through a challenge is to create some innate coping strategies beforehand so that when a crisis arises in the future, some areas of life can still function efficiently. The ways in which a person copes during a crisis will form valuable stepping stones to the revival of one's being afterward. It can be extremely hard to think of what can be done to survive when something dreadful, or even inconceivable happens, but it is not impossible.

Most families experience some kind of heartbreak and overcome many challenges on a regular basis, but the real question is, "How does one 'bounce back' after going through more complex, stressful, and often unfathomable experiences?", especially when some effects and impacts can often be felt for many years to come. It is important to have some ways to keep the family going as much as possible during hard times and during times when ideas, resilience, perseverance, or solutions won't come to fruition easily. Adolescence can be problematic and create challenges within a family. Whether teenagers are pushing boundaries, exploring relationships, or trying things that parents hoped they wouldn't, managing a family or running a household during these "experiments" can be extremely difficult and stressful. Therefore, having some things in place for when nobody has the energy, time, or ability to rationalize in the thick of it all is critical in keeping some order in the chaos. Changes and additives to every day or usual family routines need to be unique to each family and subtle in that the processes are easy, maintainable and create some kind of relief. This relief may be in the way of buying some time, looking after the health of family members, or lightening the load on all as the challenge is navigated and managed.

Having work shifts on a calendar, regular washing days, buying groceries online, exploring flexible work arrangements, and allocating and enforcement of small chores to teenagers can be useful family practices during a crisis. As is having some continuity in the less demanding tasks such as someone walking a dog, putting the bins out, emptying the dishwasher, and the like. Sharing the load on a day-to-day basis and having family members organized in this way will help to keep the household functioning when challenges arise. It is a bit like when your computer has processes running in the background that are making your machine work more effectively. We don't need to think about what the computer or family is doing constantly; it is just happening as it should, and as a result, things are running more smoothly and efficiently. Even if the family member who undertakes the task is out of action, it is easy for another member to know where they have to pick up the slack. Being organized and consistent can really be a lifesaver.

Feeling sick, getting injured, or becoming terminally ill can have a huge impact on a person's life, not to mention the lives of their friends and family. Unfortunately, illness affects people in different ways so it can be hard to know how to manage oneself, let alone a family, career, or relationship during the period of an illness. COVID-19 is a good example of how the same illness can affect people in different ways. Some people who contracted the disease were bed-bound and fighting for their lives, while others didn't even know they had it. Receiving a life-threatening diagnosis and enduring the pain and treatment throughout that journey can be a very harrowing experience. Many people are traumatized and frightened, not knowing how to cope with the possibility of long-term pain and suffering or, even worse, death as their prognosis. There is also the issue of diseases that come back, especially to those who feel as though they can't do it again. What those people go through and the emotions, pain, and upheaval it brings is unimaginable for most. While people can't predict or plan for receiving such news, there are things people can do that can strengthen the mind and body so they are better able to think, act, and react in a more mindful way during a health crisis.

To keep on top of one's health, visiting a doctor, keeping up with vaccines, and undertaking screenings at appropriate life stages are absolutely paramount. As is seeking advice from medical professionals as soon as possible when concerned about new symptoms, existing symptoms, and worsening symptoms affecting one's well-being. Too many times, people push their ill health aside and try to carry on rather than be bothered to undertake an investigation to determine the underlying cause. Too many times, people are told either that it's too late and they can't be treated more successfully, or pass away unexpectedly as a result. If a person has any new things going on with their bodies, it is always a good idea to visit the doctor and check it out. It is equally as important to follow up after the visit as well - doing so could potentially save one's life. There are also other preventative measures that can be taken to keep one's health in check. Maintaining good nutrition, regular exercise, and getting plenty of sleep are a few staples that can help to keep major potential health problems at bay. Also, nurturing the mind through intentional mindfulness is vital in working through and managing health problems, particularly problems relating to chronic pain.

When people are experiencing challenges within their family, health, and relationships, the impacts can negatively seep into their jobs as well. This may be evident in their interactions with others, productivity levels, enthusiasm, or behavior. During a crisis, it can be very hard to process information, think clearly, or make decisions. Let's not forget that people also experience crises in their workplaces, which can have huge impacts on health, relationships, and well-being. On the contrary, work could be the only area in one's life that is stable and in order to manage a crisis, undertaking a routine and familiar activity such as work may be the only thing keeping a person going. In addition, if someone is going through a family crisis, going to work can be a good coping strategy because of the different contexts. Undertaking familiar tasks can help people to "fill their cups" during challenges, particularly at a time when their cups are empty from dealing with high-stress situations. Whether one can work or not work during a difficult time, or if the crisis is work-related or non-work-related, it is helpful for people to have some tricks up their sleeve for when appropriate decisions relating to resuming, stopping, or making changes to their work situation need to be made.

Speaking to close work colleagues and supervisors about present hardships can help some people feel at ease about their decision to resume or stop work. When one feels empathy from others and is free of judgment, it is more likely their continuation or return to work will be successful, as the individual will be able to focus on the tasks at hand rather than get overwhelmed by social or workplace politics. If the crisis or challenges are in the workplace, it is important to engage in opportunities and processes that promote reconciliation. This may include working with management to resolve issues, seeking union assistance, utilizing counseling services, visiting a doctor to discuss mental health, having impartial conversations with friends or family, and, most importantly, reflecting on yourself to consider why the crisis has occurred, how it can be resolved and what can be done to prevent it from happening again. Reflecting on and admitting one's involvement in the challenge and taking ownership of wrongdoings is a very important part of reaching an ideal resolution.

Relationships can be very difficult to maintain at the best of times let alone during a crisis. When challenges arise, emotions spiral out of control, bodies are in "fight" or "freeze" mode and brains can misinterpret information. So, regulating oneself can be extremely hard, or at times, appear impossible to do. The dysregulation of one's behavior, actions, and reactions experienced by some can cause irreparable damage to relationships with others. Therefore, developing and sustaining positive, supportive, and loving relationships is critical for optimum health and well-being. Relationships are good for the soul as they promote fulfillment and complement one's journey through life. Hence, working towards repairing breakages and reinvigoration through concerted effort and sometimes change is key to overall success and happiness.

Communication can "make or break" a relationship and should never be underestimated. When challenges arise, it can be hard to communicate clearly or appropriately, and often people say things that they don't really mean. Similar to not being able to "unsee" something, one may not be able to "unsay" something. During a crisis or outside of one, refining how one speaks with, and to another, to ensure they do so in respectful, empathic, and supportive ways is one of the best things a person can do. Being open and vulnerable with people about feelings, worries, and problems creates a picture of love, support, and mutual respect and encourages opportunities for growth in the relationship. Seeking help from relationship professionals is also a good option to develop or polish one's communication skills. There is nothing wrong with needing support to fix present communication problems or learning about new purposeful methods to try. Doing so will improve the quality of one's life and encourage healthy, fulfilling relationships with others. When some friendships or relationships end, it can be a very upsetting time, but the situation need not be hopeless. When one is ready, there are more friendships and relationships waiting to happen.

Crisis. Challenge. Conflict. Poor health. Disease. Heartbreak. Loss. All inevitable events that happen to everyone, yet so challenging for all to accept. Experiencing a crisis, whether it be related to family, work, relationships, or health, is devastating, and can dramatically reduce the quality of one's life. Therefore, every person should prioritize looking after themselves every day, inside and out, to build the strength of mind and soul and grow the stamina needed to survive and thrive through crises and life in general. Many simple things can be done, one step at a time, when a person is ready to move forward. Spending time reflecting on oneself, and making necessary adjustments and changes needed to prepare for life's challenges can make a big difference rather than letting oneself be defeated by them. Organization is an important 'buzzword' as it helps alleviate some stress during hard times. Enhancing one's communication skills and building healthy, trusting, and supportive relationships with others is a necessity. Everyone needs the right people in their corner. In summation, spend endless time developing yourself and nurturing your body and mind whenever possible, in ways that are preferred by oneself. Be the captain of your ship so you can look after your crew members.

Allison Rose Clark

Founder of Tigerfly Energy Creations

https://www.linkedin.com/in/allison-rose-clark/
https://www.facebook.com/AllisonRoseClarkAuthor
https://www.instagram.com/tigerflyenergycreations_arc/
https://allisonroseclark.com.au/
https://www.smashwords.com/books/view/1288439

Allison Rose Clark lives on the South Coast of NSW Australia and is a mum of three boys and a ginger cat. During her childhood and early adulthood, she endured school bullying, child sexual abuse, domestic violence, plus other traumas. In 2018, Allison released her first book, "I Don't Hate Me Anymore", which has seen much interest and coverage through a variety of media avenues including online and offline. With a passion to see women empowered to perceive themselves in a different light, thus lifting them out of childhood survival mechanisms and destructive mental habits. Allison successfully attained a Diploma in Counselling while studying at Wollongong TAFE as well as achievements in suicide prevention and domestic violence courses. Allison also regularly makes efforts to improve her personal growth. Some goals of Allison's include writing further books and continue spreading the message of loving oneself completely without compromising through speaking opportunities.

IT STARTED WHEN....

By Allison Rose Clark

PANIXIOUS PLEA

Calm my anxious
Spirit.
Still my racing
Thoughts.
Give me peace
Within my heart.
Make worry
Take a stroll.
Let desperation
Drift away
Like currents
Carry water.
Relax my body
And my mind.
Some things
I can't control.

Written by Allison Rose Clark 2014©

"Recovery is possible for everyone, no matter how hopeless a situation may seem" —Ruth C. White.

I grew up in a relatively normal household. That is, one full of your usual dysfunction of parents arguing and siblings squabbling; a rollercoaster of emotions and behaviors which saw you get angry over nothing and then be loving for every reason (sometimes to overkill levels).

Everyone lugs around some level of trauma which comes out in times of overwhelm. Some they own and some they inherit. Every generation carries the traumas of the previous generation, handed down unknowingly from their parents to them. This is known as "vicarious trauma". The children then grow up with their parents' trauma through their parenting decisions/indecisions. In turn, they add their own trauma to their own children. Hence, a cycle of vicarious trauma is carried from one generation to the next until it's broken.

This cycle affects everyone on some level, including mentally. With trauma comes the health of our minds. How have your experiences impacted your thoughts towards yourself and others, your life, what's important and what isn't, morals and values? In turn, how have those impacted your perceptions and understandings of the world, how you interact with others, your emotions and reactions, and the levels they go to? In what ways have these experiences affected your choices throughout your life? Have you repeated your parents' upbringing of you, or have you used it as a source of strength to change the way you live and parent? Therefore continuing, or breaking, the cycle.

Much of what people experience as adults originates from their childhood. They developed coping mechanisms which helped them to survive situations and circumstances they were too young to comprehend, were scary, or were in danger of being hurt. As adults, people still experience those survival techniques. Only now, those responses are not needed anymore. The person no longer needs to be protected from what they don't understand. New strategies to face the future are what are needed.

My life journey is scattered with many kinds of trauma. Child sexual abuse, school bullying from ages seven to seventeen, domestic violence times four (married to three), attempted rape and attempted murder, harassment, and intimidation, being used as a scapegoat way too many times, and being blamed for things I never did or said. Some of these were perpetrated by family, some from friends, and some from people I never knew.

The thing my psychologist noticed was how my parents raised my siblings and me. There had been no addictions, abuse, or any other family characteristic that would normally accompany someone's trauma. What made my psychologist think this was an interesting point? All my experiences were from outside the family unit. Home was always our sanctuary and a safe place for us growing up. Despite not having grown up in an abusive home, I still wound up in a similar position as someone who had. Where, in my childhood, did my trauma begin?

For me, the beginning lies with the child sexual abuse I endured at the hands of my cousin while he babysat my siblings and me. Twice. I was eight years old. Everything which followed from there compounded and was buried deep. My whole life was affected – thoughts about myself and others, my trust in men and boys, making and keeping friends, decisions I made, being fearful all the time about everything so missing opportunities. I became withdrawn and quiet when I had, previously, been energetic and outgoing, was desperate for people to like me, wanted to fix everything, felt at fault for everything which went wrong, and much more.

In 2000, when I was roughly 25 or 26 years old, the volcano erupted! And it was spectacular! My family doctor told me it was major depression, prescribed me antidepressants, and sent me home.

In 2014, after fourteen years of misdiagnosed and mistreated mental health concerns, The Black Dog Institute in Sydney, Australia, finally confirmed I had been experiencing Bi-Polar II, a panic disorder, Obsessive Compulsive Disorder (OCD), and Post-Traumatic Stress Disorder (PTSD). To date, with the correct treatments which they had recommended, I am now considered stable. I am still seeing a psychiatrist and psychologist to help me deal with my everyday life as well as triggers as they crop up.

Ever heard someone say, "I was never like this. I don't know why everything is all of a sudden falling apart. I just want to go back to how I used to be. Things were easier," or something along those lines?

These were the words of an ex-boyfriend from a few years back. He'd grown up in an abusive home. His father was an alcoholic, and he saw his mum abused many times in various ways, as was he abused along with his brother. He never had a birthday cake or party, and never asked to have friends over because he was ashamed, but his father would not allow him to see his friends anyway. School was littered with bullies who taunted him daily. It was all school, work in the shop, and loneliness for him as a child. Totally heartbreaking to hear from a person who has grown up experiencing that version of life.

My ex-boyfriend told me of the many times his mother was hit, thrown about, and the manner in which his father carried out these things. How his father broke furniture and other items, was verbally abusive, financially abusive, mentally abusive, isolated the family from other family members and friends, and the list just went on!

How this affected my ex long-term became apparent in a major way a couple of years before I met him in 2017. For over ten years, he had been estranged from his parents and brother, and for a number of years during that time, he owned his own business. While working on a project with another company, he started becoming more and more aggressive. He abused the people he was working with and was insubordinate towards those in charge. Eventually, his contract was canceled. Following on from there, broken relationships continued due to his anger, which he told me he wasn't sure where it came from. He would go from calm to super angry to calm again in a matter of minutes. It wasn't until he started seeing a psychiatrist and psychologist that he was able to recognize where it all started. Also, he realized, though ignorant of it at the time, that he had always had issues regarding authority. The mental health conditions my ex was diagnosed as having were Bipolar II and PTSD.

What my ex learned was that all of this stemmed from his childhood and impacted him through how he saw the world, others, his relationships, his behavior, others' behaviors, and his perception of right and wrong regarding his own thoughts, words, and actions, how intensely he felt his emotions and the extent those feelings were expressed. He appeared to be a calm and harmless man when we met. However, when we moved in together, his whole demeanor and attitude changed. He became abusive in the same manner he had described his father had treated his mother. My ex told me because we were living together he got to tell me what to do, how to dress, etc. Obviously, he believed he had the right to control everything in our relationship, and expected me to ask his permission before undertaking anything.

The purpose of sharing these stories is to show how a person's upbringing has a huge impact on their mental health and the effects upon their life, some for the rest of their lives. Both my ex and I experienced childhood at home very differently. Our school years were similar in regards to being bullied. The relationships we'd been in had been volatile. Regardless, each of our differing experiences resulted in, but aren't limited to, mental health concerns, harmful decision-making, and unhealthy relationship dynamics, friendships included. When my ex and I ended our relationship, I wasn't angry. I felt compassion and was understanding of his brokenness. With his continued treatment, I was hopeful for him in all his future endeavors.

When it came to my life experiences and how they affected me, I was able to pinpoint many things.

My tendency to feel responsible and always wanting to fix everything was a result of my cousin sexually assaulting me. This is where all my trauma started, further compounded with each and every event or incident thereafter. That experience made me feel extremely responsible, guilty, and ashamed of what happened to my sisters and me. The blame, I'd decided, sat with me. Also, I felt silenced, defeated, unconfident, and fearful. He'd taken from me my spark, leaving me shy, withdrawn, and quiet - the perfect bully victim.

Bullying led to hating myself, reinforced the shame I felt, kept me silent, continued to feed my lack of confidence, compounded the insecurity and fear of rejection I'd developed, and excelled in the growth of desperation to be liked.

After my cousin destroyed the lives of my sisters and myself, I never felt safe. I needed to feel in control of what was happening to me. Due to his actions, I realized I couldn't control what others did to me, but I could control my environment. Enter OCD and PTSD. Once, after learning what OCD and PTSD were, and being able to relate to the signs and symptoms, I inquired concernedly of a workshop facilitator if my experiences could be either of these. She asked me if they were affecting my life. I responded, "Not at the moment." Her response was, matter-of-factually, "It couldn't possibly be those because they aren't affecting your life." I believed her.

Growing up, mental health wasn't a big topic. It wasn't until I was married to my first husband, which is when I had my breakdown, that I started to learn about it. I was diagnosed with major depression at that particular time. That was the diagnosis for any depression which lasted more than two weeks. I was treated for such with medication, which for the most part didn't seem to work. Counseling wasn't mentioned.

For years, I'd asked my doctor about the things happening to me. Even asked if it could be manic depression. "No," he would tell me, and proceed to tell me why. Obviously, I took him for his word as, indeed, my signs and symptoms didn't line up with those of manic depression. It did leave me bewildered, though, because I felt all over the place. Regardless, I accepted it to be normal. Unbeknownst to me, decades later, the medical industry divided manic depression into two categories - Bipolar I and Bipolar II.

During my third marriage, my mental health reached an all-time low. Suicidal thoughts were constant. It honestly felt like I was losing my mind! I even considered admitting myself to the mental health ward at the local hospital! The clinical psychologist I was seeing then suggested what I was experiencing may be more than depression. So, she suggested the Black Dog Institute (Sydney, Australia). The testing they put me through was extensive and thorough. Conducted in batches, it was a total of five hours of questions and consultation. At the end of the assessment, the psychiatrist wrote a detailed report and gave suggestions for ongoing medications and treatment. It was from the Black Dog Institute that I was given my diagnosis, confirming some of which I'd suspected for a very long time.

What did I do with this information, you may ask?

Well, the right medication helped me to think clearer and balance my emotions so I was able to see my life from a different perspective. Due to my marriage being abusive, I started considering what I was doing, what I was allowing, and why I was doing those things. Almost all my life has been spent in fear. I realized my thinking about myself and my life influenced my mental health immensely, thus impacting my actions, reactions, decisions, and indecisions.

Over the past nine years, the growth I have experienced within myself has been exponential!

Nearly all of my trauma is associated with my childhood. Knowing where it started made it easier to tackle the roots of the weed which had entangled itself within my soul and spirit. If you were to try to find out where your trauma started, I would recommend making sure you have someone you can talk to, such as a counselor. This is because the emotional scars which will likely be triggered may be overwhelming for you. Once you have discovered your weed, pull it out by the roots by acknowledging and accepting your past. Easier said than done, I know. That's why you need a counselor.

Another thing I did which helped my mental health was reminding myself of what is good in my life and about myself. It's not as easy as it sounds. Much of what I could think of was negative. That's because when you're depressed, your mind is more focused on what's going wrong. By doing that, my attitude and perception of myself and my life slowly shifted, releasing the decades-dense heaviness from my shoulders and off my mind.

Would you like to experience a more positive outlook on life?

Now, being positive isn't about ignoring reality. Life throws you a curveball sometimes. Having a positive perspective allows you to cope better with events by keeping despair to a minimum and reminding yourself the situation is temporary.

How did I achieve this positive attitude, you ask?

In a notebook, I tried to list ten things I liked about myself and ten things which were positive in my life. Despite these sounding like the same thing, they're not. "About myself" relates to aspects of your being such as hair, talents, and personality. "In my life" relates to those around you such as your children, environment, and occupation.

May I encourage you to create lists of your own? It's one step you can take today towards the betterment of your mental health.

Once I had compiled my lists, I designed illustrated documents which I then displayed on my lounge room wall so I could be reminded of them every day. I invite you to do the same with your lists. You're limited only by the creativeness of your own imagination. Consider art, painting, drawing, or designing a poster. If you enjoy writing, maybe put your lists into a poem or a letter to your younger self.

I would be honored if you were to decide to share with me how you have traveled using these methods.

Persistence with consistency will serve you well.

Dori Mekhiche

Founder of Yumswitch

https://www.linkedin.com/in/dori-mekhiche-8ab3038
https://www.facebook.com/profile.php?id=100085306771940
https://www.instagram.com/just.breathe.by.yumswitch/
https://yumswitch.com

In my journey from the dynamic world of the Financial Services Industry, where I honed my skills in Marketing and Communications, I've evolved into a dedicated advocate for holistic well-being and personal transformation. With a passion for guiding individuals toward greater health and healing, I've become a Certified Trauma-Informed Breathwork Facilitator and Certified Health Coach.

Trauma-Informed Breathwork: Drawing from my background, I've seamlessly transitioned into the realm of Trauma-Informed Breathwork. By providing a safe and compassionate space, I empower individuals to explore the profound healing power of their breath. Together, navigating the pathways to release stress, process trauma, and find renewal, fostering emotional resilience and inner balance.

Holistic Health Coaching: I also work collaboratively with clients to transform their lifestyles, incorporating mindful nutrition, joyful movement, stress management, and self-care. My approach is personalized and empathetic, supporting clients to achieve their wellness goals with sustainable changes.

TURNING ADVERSITY INTO A CATALYST FOR CHANGE

By Dori Mekhiche

In the heart of the Financial Services Industry where deadlines, travel, commuting, and meetings dictated the rhythm of my life, an unexpected twist of fate awaited. Little did I know that my path would lead me from the fast-paced world of marketing and communications to the serene realm of holistic well-being and personal transformation. My story is one of battling to become a mom against the odds while focusing on my career, turning adversity into a catalyst for change, and emerging as a dedicated advocate for health and healing.

Chapter 1: Entrenched in the Dynamic

The world of Financial Services was my crucible where I honed my skills in marketing and communications. The fast-paced environment, business travel to places like London, Bermuda, and the United States along the East Coast, West Coast, and in between alongside the relentless pursuits of targets, and the constant buzz of being busy also became my daily companions. Amid the completed projects and deadlines and travel, I found a sense of accomplishment, yet the demands of this world while trying to become a mom at the same time eventually took their toll. I experienced recurring losses while having to bounce back rather quickly. I grieved briefly and then bounced back to the task at hand: my career. There was not a lot of room for thinking or grieving; I only had time to be sad, wonder why this was happening to me, and then get back to work because I did not want to stand out, show any emotional weakness, or be the center of attention. I also needed a distraction. After multiple times of enduring a loss, I knew that I stood out in my group. I knew that people knew. I always felt it would be different the next time, but each time I heard the expression from a doctor's office, "Be cautiously optimistic," my positivity turned to fear. When was this going to end? This was not the battle that I expected or envisioned. I felt like I was in the trenches, up to my neck drowning, and prayed for a way out. As I heard news stories about people mistreating children and being left in cars, I grew sadder internally. I was left wondering what I had done to deserve this amount of pain, why me? I realized that many other women did not have the challenge I was experiencing, even the ones that according to most values didn't deserve the opportunity to bring life into the world. Something that was meant to be so beautiful became sad. Here is my story.

Chapter 2: Unveiling the Challenge

Within one year, at the age of 34, I relocated from NYC to Boston, leaving behind a career as divisional vice president of marketing, started a career in a new city at a company with a different culture, got engaged, started building a new home, and got married. As the curtain rose on this new chapter in my personal life, I was blindsided by the challenge that would change everything. Amid the rewards of accomplishment, a different kind of battle was quietly unfolding within me. The demands of my corporate life seemed to clash with the demands of my body, creating an intricate web of stress and uncertainty.

Chapter 3: The Seeds of Transformation

Amid the chaos, a whisper of transformation emerged. My struggle with reproductive challenges became the catalyst for change. It was a turning point that shifted my perspective, compelling me to explore avenues beyond the corporate walls. The seeds of holistic well-being were planted as I, unbeknownst to myself at the time, embarked on a journey of self-discovery and healing. Hot, Chinese herbal medicine drinks on the way to the train in the morning that I substituted for coffee and gluten-free diets were not providing the success that I had hoped for. For many, I am sure they have, but not for me. At the age of 39, I ended my career.

Chapter 4: From Challenge to Compassion

The walls of the Financial Services Industry, once stressful, began to crumble. I began to explore my creative side. I connected with a bunch of warm-hearted ladies while diving into a weekly pottery & ceramics class. That connection and creativity expanded into my passion for interior decorating, and from there, I was tapped to work at a well-known high-end home design store. One of my colleagues there knew about my reproductive challenges and recommended that I try the Japanese art of Reiki.

Because I was not one to let the grass grow under my feet, I immediately made an appointment. Over time, I realized that I manifested a beautiful, loving, caring, and kind support team. The Reiki practitioner shared the name of an acupuncturist, and together they were on a mission to help however they could. Together, we explored various holistic approaches, seeking not only to address the physical aspect of my struggle, but also to nourish my soul and spirit.

Chapter 5: The Power of Community

As the days turned into weeks, and the weeks into months, I found solace in this newfound community. The pottery and ceramics class became a medium of expression, a tangible representation of my journey. Each piece I created held a story, a piece of my heart and soul embedded within the curves and edges.

The high-end home design store transformed into a sanctuary, a space where I could channel my creativity and share it with others. It was there that I met individuals who had their own battles, their own triumphs. We formed a network of support, a tapestry of shared experiences and mutual understanding.

The practice of Reiki became a beacon of light, a source of comfort during moments of doubt and despair. Through gentle touch and healing energy, I felt a profound sense of connection to my own body, a rekindling of trust in its wisdom.

The acupuncturist, with his skilled hands and ancient knowledge, provided a path to balance and harmony, guiding me toward a state of wellness that extended beyond the physical realm.

In these moments of vulnerability, I discovered a strength within myself that I had never known before. It was a transformation that went far beyond the confines of my reproductive challenges. It was a rebirth of my spirit, a blossoming of compassion and self-love that would lay the foundation for the chapters yet to come.

Chapter 6: The Final Quest

With newfound determination coursing through my veins, I stood at the threshold of a monumental decision. I found myself ready to conquer trying to become a mom one last time.

Gathering the lessons of resilience and the support of my newfound tribe, I embarked on this final quest with a fierce sense of purpose. The landscape of my journey had shifted from one of despair to one of hope, from solitude to a chorus of caring souls who walked beside me.

The process was not without its challenges. There were moments of doubt, moments where fear threatened to resurface. But with every sunrise, I reminded myself of the strength that had brought me this far. I delved into every available resource, combining modern medical expertise with the ancient wisdom of holistic practices. It was a dance of science and soul, a harmonious symphony of hope and determination.

Over time, I found myself embracing each moment, treasuring the journey for what it was - a testament to the human spirit's capacity to endure, evolve, and ultimately triumph.

Chapter 7: A Blossoming

And then, one fateful morning, as the first light of dawn painted the sky in hues of pink and gold, the universe whispered its affirmation. The long-awaited moment had arrived. The seeds of hope that I had nurtured with unwavering devotion had taken root and begun to bloom.

In the embrace of this newfound life, I discovered a profound gratitude that transcended words. Every trial, every tear, had led me to this sacred juncture. It was a moment of exquisite

transformation, a testament to the power of the human spirit and the boundless capacity of the heart to love.

When I was finally able to cradle our precious bundles in my arms, I knew that this journey, with all its twists and turns, had sculpted me into a woman of unparalleled strength and compassion.

With my heart overflowing, I looked ahead to the chapters yet to be written, knowing that whatever challenges lay in wait, I was armed with the unshakable knowledge that the seeds of resilience, once planted, could weather any storm.

Through my personal journey with grief that ultimately led to success, my understanding of holistic healing deepened. With a heart ignited by compassion, I embarked on a mission to heal and one day guide others facing similar challenges. My own experiences had taught me the importance of empathy and support, and I was determined to be a beacon of light for others navigating their own struggles.

Chapter 8: The Birth of a Health Coach

My path continued to evolve, leading me to become a Certified Holistic Health Coach. Blending my expertise in marketing and communications and my weight loss journey as a mom with my newfound passion for holistic well-being, I embarked on a mission to guide individuals toward greater health and healing. The corporate skills that had once defined my identity now found a new purpose—to empower others on their journey to vitality and balance.

Chapter 9: The Trauma-Informed Breathwork Revelation

Within the folds of my personal transformation, a profound revelation awaited: Trauma-Informed Breathwork. It was through this practice that I discovered a powerful tool for healing—one that went beyond the physical and delved into the emotional and spiritual realms. As I trained to become a Certified Trauma-Informed Breathwork Facilitator, I realized that my journey was intricately intertwined with the very essence of healing that I aimed to share with the world. Ultimately, I had the "thing". A practice where I not only was able to witness helping others, but one that set my soul on fire.

Chapter 10: Embracing Transformation

As I look back on my journey—a tapestry woven with threads of struggle, growth, and resilience—I stand at the crossroads of transformation. The Financial Services Industry, where I honed my skills and faced my challenges, served as the crucible from which my true calling emerged. I am now a living testament to the power of embracing change, and of using adversity as a stepping stone toward purpose and fulfillment.

Epilogue: A New Dawn

Today, I am not only a Certified Holistic Health Coach and Certified Trauma-Informed Breathwork Facilitator; I am also a beacon of hope for those navigating their own journeys of healing. My story is a testament to the human spirit's capacity to rise above challenges, embrace transformation, and channel pain into purpose. From the corporate hustle to the serene realms of holistic well-being, I have found my true calling—to guide and empower individuals toward greater health, healing, and a life illuminated by the light of resilience.

In the tapestry of life, my journey from the Financial Services Industry to the challenges of becoming a mom, which ultimately led me to become a Certified Holistic Health Coach and Certified Trauma-Informed Breathwork Facilitator, weaves a story of courage, transformation, and empowerment. This tale showcases my evolution from adversity to advocacy, serving as an inspiration to others who may be seeking their own path to holistic well-being and personal transformation.

Krissy Emily Brooke

https://www.instagram.com/krissy.emily.brooke/

My name is Krissy, I am 28 years old. I've had a crazy journey to find myself and what lights me up. It has been filled with so many lessons, and isolation. I grew up in an unstable home, later went into foster care, and then was adopted. I've handled all the adversity that has come my way with grace, kindness, and my 6lb pomeranian Lexi by my side because trauma makes you bitter or better. My goal since I was a kid was to share my story to help inspire others and not succumb to the deep dark feelings that come from the struggles of life like overwhelming feelings of loneliness that dilute our vision, passions, and path we are meant to accomplish. I chose to be better, and I hope to inspire others to be better.

BITTER OR BETTER

By Krissy Emily Brooke

One of my favorite quotes is "Your pain either makes you bitter or better." I don't know who said it, but it has been something that has stuck with me. This is a condensed version of my messy life and how somehow I've navigated through it to not only get better, but remain a kind, caring, and loving human being at the same time.

I was born into a family that I don't know too much about because my subconscious has blocked out a significant amount of my childhood up until the age of seven. The few memories I have are of me hiding behind a couch to avoid going to school in kindergarten. Who needs to say they are sick to avoid school? Just don't be seen and they'll forget you exist. I wasn't taken care of very well; meals consisted of rotten food or flour and sugar mixed together.

By some grace of God I was apprehended and put into foster care. Somehow, I thought this was going to be better. And in some instances it was; I had proper meals, and I wasn't smacked around or choked by a belt, or whipped by anything in sight. Unfortunately, the abuse I experienced in my foster home, and later adoptive family, cut a lot deeper than malnutrition and physical wounds. It was all mental and emotional, constantly made to feel like I wasn't enough unless I did something to earn the attention or love from my guardians. I learned from a very young age how to mold into everything and anything to just be "loved" by everyone. I wasn't ever held as a child and I definitely was never told everything was going to be okay. I had to learn to comfort myself. I had to give myself a reason to keep going, keep existing, and keep putting in the daily efforts regardless of how shitty I felt. When I was a lot younger I remember sitting in my room thinking the blessing of being adopted was going to give me the ability to help so many people because I would get through all these hard times completely on my own and it wouldn't result in the typical coping mechanisms. I wouldn't drink or smoke weed or do any of the stuff a lot of other kids are doing nowadays.

I stayed sober until my worst nightmare came true. My biggest fear was having my adoptive family turn their back on me and see that I wasn't worth the effort anymore, just like they did to my oldest brother. Adopted and kicked out of the house and family by the ripe age of 15. I could only imagine how lonely that must have been for him. I still beat myself up for not being there for him and reaching out. I was a kid and unfortunately, I believed the lies they told me about him. When I was around 21 or 22, I started the hardest of my days. I attempted suicide; I took anything and everything possible. I started with 40 t3s and topped it off with a complete cocktail of antidepressants, anti-anxiety medications, cholesterol medication, diabetic medication, sleeping pills, and the list goes on. That day I felt like it didn't matter what I did because the family that chose me, the family that housed me, and fed me since I was seven years old was pulling away and making me feel a black hole of emptiness in my soul. This was the first time I felt the complete, overwhelming pain of being chosen just to be discarded like your old favorite t-shirt.

I woke up in the hospital two weeks later and the doctors had no idea how or why I was still alive. I went home and no one spoke to me for an entire month. Other than to make jokes about me killing myself again. Not long after this situation took place I was shipped to my aunt and uncle's home to help with their kids. Where my parents didn't tell them what had happened or where I was mentally. They dropped me off with all of my stuff and went back to their home. They stopped texting me, stopped calling, and eventually blocked me and changed their phone numbers. That's when my biggest fear came true. I had hit my version of rock bottom. I was fighting this echo in the back of my head that on one hand I am absolutely disposable, and on the other, if I gave in and succeeded at suicide it was a weak man's way out. So I turned to what anyone who is too down to keep living but is too afraid of ending it turns to. The sweet flavor of any alcohol to numb out the deep pit in my entire body. For months, I struggled with drinking, blacking out in the streets, waking up trying to find my car, and struggling my way to work to do it all over again. Making terrible financial decisions and not thinking clearly. I racked up over six figures of debt in one year.

One day I had a massive realization that as hurtful as everything I've been through was, nobody was going to save me and nobody was going to make sure I was taken care of because nobody cared. I know that at some point in everyone's lives, to some degree, we all feel this. It's an isolating and lonely feeling to carry with you in every attempt to do better, be better, and create better. It was at this moment that I decided, I made a conscious decision, that not only was it worth it but I was going to prove them all wrong. You not only walked out of my life and left me so low and broken but I am rising like a phoenix from the ashes. I decided I was going to pull myself out of drinking. I quit cold turkey. Isolated myself with no friends, just work and my dog.

Once I took myself and my life seriously, the people who were holding me back or not elevating me naturally fell off. It was a painful experience to lose so many people that I considered to be close. Especially as the child in me feared abandonment and being alone, I pushed that fear away and stuck to my guns to keep working on myself and my life to create a better life for myself, my dog, and the future family that I would build around me.

This dog I can honestly say saved my life. It's one thing to have the moment of strength to choose to do better and be better, but when it comes to action, it's as if you have to make that decision every single fucking day. This dog gave me hope that things were going to turn out well for me. She gave me discipline - you can not stay in bed all day wallowing in sadness and depression when you have a five-pound baby nugget who has no control of her bladder and is unable to feed herself. She gave me unconditional love. I am not perfect and have made many mistakes throughout my journey to get to where I am now. Regardless of my mistakes, I always came home to her as excited as ever to see me and giving me a million kisses. She was the first experience of unconditional love, both to receive and to give. She has given me accountability; it's easy to skip out on yourself but it's fucking hard to skip out when you have someone counting on you to show up and do the things you would rather not do.

Once I was consistent enough with showing up for her, I learned that the ways I was taught to navigate through life were not serving me, and had yet another lesson shoving its presence in my face. I was in Houston, Texas doing door-to-door sales for solar panels (more details on this experience to come). I finally hit a wall. I was forced to sit with myself for months. Not being able to work for eight months. It was challenging in more ways than I thought possible. I was tired of the patterns entering my life and tired of the way things always seemed to go. I was angry, then over time, I reflected on not only the patterns that other people were influencing in my life but also my behavior allowing those things to happen. I allowed people to walk all over me. I allowed people to decide my worthiness based on their opinions, based on all the things they got from me, and when those things weren't coming anymore, suddenly my value changed. This was something I reflected on for months, until one day I was scrolling through my phone and found the bucket list I wrote after another screaming fit my ex had with me. I left the house and went on a long drive to this lookout in the mountains outside of Jasper. I turned my cell service off and I wrote everything and anything my little heart could think of that one day.

Someway I would accomplish these things. When I wrote this list, I was isolated, beaten down, had next to no self-worth, and stayed in a toxic situation because I had no money and was afraid to demand better for myself. The first thing I wrote on the list was skydiving. I knew that there was no way I was leaving America until I accomplished that thing on my list. The fear I felt looking into what skydiving was, the risk it involved, and all the comments that I was telling myself and my friends were telling me, made me just about decide to play small and not do it.

Then, I thought more about why I was being called to go skydiving and what it represented for me. I was more ready to jump out of a plane at 14000 feet in the air strapped to a complete stranger. I saw skydiving as the ultimate shedding of who I was before. The person who allowed people to walk in and out of my life as they pleased. The person who didn't see her worth unless it came from the lens of other people who didn't know even ⅛ of the experiences I've overcome. I was shedding the sad child in me who just wanted to be loved and accepted. In shedding all the things that were no longer serving me, I took on the role of becoming the parent and person I so desperately was searching for. Someone who loved me and accepted all the quirks and struggles that came with me. I accepted the person I was deep in my soul. That person despite all the traumas, letdowns, loss of hope, hurt, and disappointment my journey has given me. It gave me the ultimate strength. It gave me the ability to move through this broken painful world we live in with grace, an overwhelming amount of love, and understanding for other people. It gave me the ability to not only resonate and feel life to such a deep level but also the ability to feel closely to what other people are feeling so they don't feel isolated or alone. Sometimes, the only tool we need to move on from a struggle or hardship is not to be told "I understand", but to just allow that person to be seen. Saying, "I can see how hard things have been for you, and despite how hard it was you've persevered anyway. Despite all the darkness trying to take over your soul, you still treat others with kindness and respect."

Before moving back to Canada, I sold my car. Becoming debt-free in Canada, paying off over six figures in less than five years, and completely on my own.

I am a completely different person and my mindset has changed immensely, now more aligned with where I am going and not focused on where I came from. I know everyone has a story, hardships, self-doubts, and limiting beliefs that hold us back. I am no exception. I looked for ways to push my journey forward to the place and things I was destined to accomplish. One is writing a book full of all the details to inspire so many people. This chapter is just the beginning for me. And just the beginning of the lives I aspire to impact, touch, and help change.

J.R. Stephenson

Self-Employed
Coach/Counselor

Retired Educator and Special Education Counselor. Married with five adult children between my husband and myself and several grandchildren. I love traveling, contemporary jazz music, fishing with my husband on his boat, and meeting my best girlfriends for lunch and sharing. I am a Christian and very active in my church's hospitality ministry. I am passionate about children and helping the homeless population by making "Survival Sacs" with a bit of food and money to help them along their journey. I am going to begin a Dog Therapy group and give support to others in facilities and school for emotional support.

AFTER THE OUTCRY! WHAT A PARENT OR GUARDIAN SHOULD DO WHEN YOUR WORST FEARS ARE CONFIRMED!

By J.R. Stephenson

Twenty-five years ago, I couldn't have imagined that today I would be happily married to a wonderful man, in a comfortable home with three independent, educated (now adult) children along with two wonderful sons who are my extended family. I am truly now living my best life!

However, this has come out of a tragic nightmare which ended my previous marriage abruptly and the lifestyle I thought I had planned so carefully. How could I believe that such a terrible thing could happen in my life? But, yes, this incident, this horrible experience even happened to me! I had been very naive and assumed that this type of situation only happened to others. I had been careful, purposeful, and guarded with my child from my previous marriage. I only eased up with the tight control as the sole manager after years of watching and observing anyone who came into our world and home. Then eventually, it happened when I was comfortable and let my guard down and began to trust that the adult I brought into my home was safe.

After all of the caution, my child and I were the victims of a slow, purposeful plan of attack that victimized us in our own home. He began slowly grooming my child while I was not aware and taking advantage of times when I was not present to begin molesting and eventually abusing my child. In the years that followed the outcry, I would have many nights of self-reflection also feeling hatred, remorse, and anger toward the perpetrator and berating myself as to why I didn't suspect this ugly truth sooner and perhaps I could have prevented it all. But, I realized (with counseling) that I couldn't continue to blame myself for not thinking the way a pedophile thinks. How could I understand people like this with their evil agendas, their sinister or sneaky thoughts, and weaknesses which slowly creep into their sick psyche until their needs and desires take them over, and then they act on those impulses? I now understand better, because I am a mentally well adult, that I would never plan or plot to attack innocent victims. I don't have a secret agenda. Slowly, I stopped the cycle of mentally blaming myself and why I was unable to prevent this crime against my family. But, the abusers wait until victims and their families least expect it, and appear comfortable with them in their roles, and then they attack and begin to act out when you have let your guard down and have given your trust to them with your loved one.

Why would I or you ever think that someone in your innermost circle of friends, relatives, and yes even a spouse or a parent, Priest or Pastor, even a grandparent, brother, or cousin could ever do the unthinkable to you or your precious child? These are people who unfortunately get through to victims that are usually most accessible. Via relationships they establish with you through the space they hold in your life and their close relationship which is least suspect for any inappropriateness. Because of the predator's label as a friend, neighbor, cousin, coach, mentor, etc. These trusted people have great value and usually appear safe around children, family members, and their parents.

How can these abusers defame, defile, and soil these labels of honor they hold in their cherished relationships with such disrespect? Of course, who can think as they do? Broken, with sick thought patterns, individuals who have no pity for their prey, or the countless lives they touch by the unveiling of their evil works and uncanny lack of remorse or even understanding of why they should be blamed for what they have done. Or, do they have any idea of the human pain they've caused and the broken paths which are forever changed and redirected? Usually not! Rarely do they admit responsibility or blame for what they have done.

This is my story, or it could be your story. It only matters that you've experienced the harm of your precious child. Especially when it is sexual abuse, it is so ugly and unspeakable but if this happens you are required to act! Act fast! Think logically, and plan quickly to save your child, the innocent one, the victim, from any further pain. You have to stop it (the abuse) immediately (now) and not tomorrow! Prioritize your child first, you will need to put your needs last for now. It is all about helping the child or family member through this incident. Step up to the plate, be strong (find the strength), and/or look for help from a close, trusted friend or relative to walk with you on this important path. Definitely, you will need support from the legal system. Call the police and file a report immediately after the outcry. There is no time to waste. You don't want any lack of immediate action to cast an inappropriate light on you. Yes, you will be scrutinized by all legal stakeholders and the Child Protective Agency if they are involved early on, and you can't risk losing custody of your child. This would traumatize the child and you even more.

Get the predator out of your house, or you and the child "should" leave immediately and keep that secret. Seek a trusted family member or a friend to help and one you can confide in and who will be supportive of you and your child. Ask them to keep it private, until the predator is arrested or charged and file for a restraining order immediately to document your legal right to keep the abuser away from you and your child so the police can also enforce it. Don't hide the evil that has been done, it will only return to incriminate you in some sick way or give the abuser a chance to do their evil deed again. If you were in a relationship with the abuser, I have to say it should now be over! As soon as you are aware of the terrible actions you will never be able to mend your relationship with that person, and if you are in a relationship with that person don't even try to go back! It is very difficult to accept that perhaps someone you loved and trusted will never be allowed in your company or that of your child under normal circumstances. You will need to be strong; you won't understand how it happened and the abuser will plead and say perhaps they are sorry. But, how can you allow a simple apology to suffice for something as evil as this crime?

Through my belief in Jesus Christ, I was eventually able to find forgiveness. But, never again would I have a relationship with the abuser. Nor would I suggest it to anyone who experiences this, particularly if it was with your child. It sends a very bad connotation to your healing victim that in some way you were okay with what the perpetrator did and children aren't mature enough to understand the rekindling of this relationship and you have to be strong enough to sever that tie. It is a wound that never heals for the victim. Try to pull strength from your higher power to pull you through this because it will be months and perhaps years waiting for the trial and other situations to settle down i.e. relocating and rebuilding your life or changing jobs and becoming economically stable if you suffer the loss of additional income for support. The forgiveness is more for you than the abuser, "Vengeance is mine saith the Lord," you don't want the hate and anger to fester like cancer from within; it will make you sick. Don't neglect family and personal counseling, it is vital for your mental healing. Go through with all that is required to persecute the abuser in the legal system. This is a federal crime punishable by law. There are groups like the Crime Victims' Witness Protection Agency that can offer support. This group actually helped me supplement my childcare costs and purchased all of the gifts under my Christmas tree the first year of my separation before my divorce. Money was very tight and I was so overwhelmed with gratitude at the generosity. When you make sure that the abuser is punished you might just prevent another unsuspecting victim from this tragedy!

I will go through the steps from my personal experiences that a parent or guardian should take if you are ever a victim of this particular crime. My goal is to help others in any way I can to prevent the harming of any child and or one of your family members from going through this. Unfortunately, I know that there's more of a need nowadays for these practical tips than I'd like to admit. Unfortunately, in today's society, these incidents are occurring more often than in the past. So, it is with reluctance that I write these tips, hoping it will help to heal others who experience this crime against their child and family and how to get through it.

I also want to add to the end of my story: "I helped to prosecute the perpetrator who committed the crime against my family and he spent five years in prison and had to register as a Sex Offender." My child grew up to be a wonderful adult and a successful person in society. I hope these tips are supportive to others in this situation or to readers who know of this situation and can help to protect the innocent and aid them in getting the victims to a place of healing and hope that a brighter day will come.

THE OUTCRY!

- The most shocking realization, the ugly truth, is when the victim comes to you with the truth, you may feel the need to disbelieve it, but follow your gut instinct and trust that you know your child and process what they are saying to you. Your first thought may be "I want to kill!" (But don't!) Begin to plan the very next step and how you will get your child out of proximity of the abuser, and yourself and/or the rest of your family to a safe house with privacy now!

- Get control of yourself! Pray, call a hotline, someone neutral not related to the abuser or you.

- Seek emotional support for the victim. Take the child to the hospital. File a police report. It is uncomfortable but they have trained professionals to take the child's statement and will refer you and the child to the correct health professionals. It is important to collect the evidence with fidelity. The hospital will do a thorough exam perhaps even a rape kit. But, continue to assure the child they did nothing wrong and you will fix this and put a stop to what is happening to them. Just continue to tell them you love them and things will get better.

- Use your critical thinking skills and go into action on where you need to move to get the child away from the abuser in secret. Make a list. You will need to process whether you need to make provisions for help i.e. reliable childcare if you still need to work, transportation if needed travel arrangements, and/or finances for your relocation. Whatever plans you make, be careful that you don't upset the child, remain as calm as you can, and don't talk in front of them when you are making plans or discussing the issue on the phone. Continue to keep the child in a harmonious environment as much as possible so you can get help and figure out your next steps to stabilize your situation. Stay home from work, if needed, and/or leave the area. Make sure you have some finances to sustain your family if possible

- Remove any contact with the abuser or from anyone who may be sympathetic to them (you would be surprised who will support the abuser). Including the school, don't inform them of what is happening but remove, if possible, the abuser from the pickup list of guardians or take legal action with a restraining order to protect the child. Update your contact list with anyone who needs to know and the school.

- Talk to immediate family in the home or environment, interview them, discuss what they know, and explain what has happened. Seek counseling for them as well and let them know it was not their fault they are victims as well.

- After filing a police report, be prepared to follow their directives; remember, all evidence is important and crucial to this case. You need to be available for their contacts and calls to discuss this crime and make sure it is done as privately as possible. All of the evidence will be turned over to the District Attorney who will decide whether to procure the abuser for this crime and they will file in court. If this happens the abuser will be arrested and will need representation. That will not be your worry. Let them go through this process on their own. You worry about the child and the many other priorities that will be stacking up. Get an attorney if you are able, or the court will appoint one for you.

- If you are married to the abuser, file for divorce. This is an abrupt end to your relationship and you will feel like you have been hit with a ton of bricks. However, you will not ever be able to resolve this and deal with your emotions. Seek immediate counseling.

Don't change your mind! You may still have feelings for the abuser but put your child and their safety above them and yourself! The child does not deserve this!

- Talk to your child calmly and explain that you are not angry with them and what was done inappropriately to them. You will have to reprogram many of their thoughts by explaining the truth (keep in mind the abuser may have been grooming them for quite some time and has threatened action if they tell or lie to them about many things).

- Allow your child to talk with the police and take personnel - they may want to interview the child alone (to make sure their story is not changed by you or the feeling involved in the trauma).

- Continue to tell your child you love them and you are sorry this happened, but you will fix it.

- Only talk to one trusted relative or friend until you have moved your child and the family is safe.

- Do not share any information about this with your co-workers or your employer!

- Get counseling at school and/or alert the nurse about any trauma and support needs for the child. "Don't talk to any unnecessary people."

- Change your child's school if necessary - pull them out of activities that may have exposed them to the abuser.

- Stay away from busy-body family gossiping friends who want the details, don't believe it, or won't keep this confidential!

- Block calls from the abuser and don't answer the calls, make sure they are aware you have a restraining order and will use it by calling the police.

- Stay off social media, do not air your thoughts publicly. Protect your child and their privacy, don't leek emotional drama on social media to tip others you are in a crisis. Keep a lid on it! This is a legal matter now!

- Seek immediate counseling for the victim and yourself and your family if needed.

- Change your surroundings and don't blame yourself for trusting a villain.

- Continue to rebuild your life and take time to get your child to heal and trust again. Teach them how to arm themselves with safe words and actions so they will not be victimized again. Rebuild self-esteem and appropriateness with their bodies.

- Do not begin any new romantic relations in or around your child's environment - this is a sacrifice and you need comforting too, but wait. Don't seek out another relationship. You are still vulnerable and may find that you've had someone who is taking advantage of this season in your life. Go slow, it takes time and you can be the bigger person to be private for a while and show your child he or she is safe at home. You will trust again but let your child help by telling you how they feel and before you bring a mate into their safe house. You will have to divulge what happened to you and your family to anyone you are considering a close relationship with because this incident will affect you and probably change your outlook on life.

- Reconnect with your higher power! Take time to invest in yourself, and make all attempts to recharge! Find time to rebuild yourself and stabilize financially. Find pleasure in the little things and joy will return. Life will get better again!

Prudence Hatchett

PH Counseling, LLC
Mental Wellness Specialist

www.linkedin.com/in/prudencehatchett/
https://www.facebook.com/phcounselingllc
PH Counseling, LLC: https://www.phcouseling.org
Learn with Prudence: https://learn-with-prudence.myshopify.com/

Prudence Hatchett earned a BA in Psychology (2004) and a M.S. in Special Education with a concentration in Emotional Disability (2006) from Mississippi State University. She earned a M.Ed. in Counselor Education (2015) and completed the master level Emotional Disability Endorsement Program in Education (2017) from the University of Mississippi. She is a National Certified Counselor (NCC), Licensed Professional Counselor (LPC) & Board Qualified Supervisor (LPC-S), Board Certified Telemental Health Provider (BC-TMH), and a Board Certified Coach (BCC). She was recently named a Subject Matter Expert (SME) for the National Board of Certified Counselors, Inc. and Affiliates. Prudence opened her own private practice, PH Counseling, LLC in 2018, which provides a variety of services including counseling, coaching, consultations, clinical supervision, and education. She holds a Master's level AA educator's license with educational endorsements in the areas of Guidance Counseling, Mild/Moderate Disabilities, Emotional Disability, and Psychology.

FROM MENTAL FATIGUE TO EMOTIONAL BREAKTHROUGH

By Prudence Hatchett

I have undoubtedly grown to be a champion, cheerleader, and advocate for all things mental health, including teaching about creating positive behavioral change and understanding brain development. Throughout my professional career, I have noticed there are specific phrases that people will repeat consistently across the board. These phrases include: "What is wrong with me?" "Why do I feel this way?" or "Why do I behave this way?" These common questions leave me to conclude that people are on a quest to feel heard, to feel better, and to feel stronger. People are seeking a way to find their own paths towards experiencing an emotional breakthrough.

According to the World Health Organization (WHO), mental health is a state of mental well-being that enables people to cope with the stresses of life, understand their own abilities, learn with intention, work well, and contribute to their community. I believe mental health, emotional wellness, and behavioral well-being are all essential parts that help increase a person's overall quality of life. Unfortunately, there are many things that take our attention away from our health, often leaving us feeling drained and depleted by the end of the day. If this occurs, mental fatigue may start to surface and intensify over time.

In this fast-paced world, we are often bombarded with the need to be in a rush and pump out responsibilities with swift action as if we were on a conveyor belt. But what happens when we continue to pour out into the world without finding balance or replenishment? We may become exhausted, feel drained, or experience a lack of energy. Without replenishment, we risk the chance of becoming so accustomed to these feelings that it becomes harder and harder to recognize that we are not supposed to feel this way. Unfortunately, these harsh feelings can become a part of everyday life. Then, if a behavior becomes normal, why should we try to improve it?

The answer lies within two important factors that are interconnected: mental and physical health. The state of our mental health can affect the state of our physical health. The state of our physical health can affect the state of our mental health. The concept is simple enough but can be difficult to manage when the dysfunction of the two health paths becomes the norm. So, what should we do about it? First, let's understand that the feeling of fatigue or exhaustion is not productive nor should it be a daily norm. When we are unaware of the state of our health, one problem will usually breed another.

It is a great idea to create time for a brain-break, a time to refocus and recharge. It's not only ok, but it is recommended to set aside time to do nothing or engage in a pleasurable activity that does not involve school or work. As I work full-time and own a business, I have plenty of projects on my plate. I love being creative and coming up with ideas to share with other people, but I also create time for self-care and rest. Meaning, I create the time to replenish, refocus, and recharge. I intentionally block off time in my schedule to just have the freedom to sit at home, watch a movie, or take a long nap. Also, it is imperative that you get enough sleep. There are countless research studies that identify the benefits of a healthy sleep routine. Your mind and body will thank you. Plus, your productivity level will skyrocket when your mind is well-rested. I truly believe that rest is a superpower!

Another important factor to consider when fighting against mental fatigue is the concept of healing. Healing is a deeper yearning for peace that comes from within an individual. Inner peace helps a person perceive things more clearly, feel things more realistically, and enhance the thought process to create a more balanced perception of life. However, if there is a hindrance to the healing process, this can prologue mental fatigue. This hindrance can include being afraid to confront certain thoughts and feelings, therefore causing you to suppress or ignore opportunities for an emotional breakthrough. To create an emotional breakthrough, one must be willing to cultivate a growth mindset. Through valid and persistent effort in the growth process, one can learn to trust their own emotions to lead them to a place of true healing. When we are willing to learn how to process our thoughts, we are choosing to grow, transform, and evolve into a higher level of self.

The brain is hard-wired for memory recall and learning new information. This new information, when properly implemented, is how humans and the world evolve and sustain society. Evolving is necessary for positive change and for the progression of life. Think about it. What if schools, families, or technology didn't evolve? Everything and everyone would be the same. No change would take place; therefore, growth would be nonexistent. During the growth process, it is natural for a person to feel more optimistic about themselves and their abilities to create positive changes. Positivity tends to breed more positivity, and more importantly, positivity can breed hope.

According to Wikipedia, the definition of hope is "an optimistic state of mind that is based on an expectation of positive outcomes with respect to events and circumstances in one's life or the world at large." As a verb, its definitions include "expect with confidence" and "to cherish a desire with anticipation." I like to think of hope as the anticipation of something positive happening. Sometimes hope can mean something simple, such as hoping that the train does not make me late for work in the morning. Other times, hope can carry a deeper meaning such as hoping for the approval of a bank loan for your first home. Either way, hope carries a positive connotation that signals satisfaction or pleasure of some kind.

Some people may argue that it is more difficult to remain hopeful when negativity or harsh circumstances are at the forefront of one's life. It is harder to see the light at the end of the tunnel when the tunnel is filled with despair. If this is the case, then how does one gain hope? According to Psychology Today, there isn't necessarily a specific formula to follow, but there are special ways to seek out hope. Consider a few basic tips including research and discovering a clear path forward, looking for role models who have found solutions, seeking out a higher power or spiritual guidance, or implementing what you already know to be true for the situation (i.e., brainstorming).

Because of its interconnectedness to the rest of the body, mental health wellness often affects other parts of the overall being. For example, have you ever heard that weight loss starts in the mind? Or that meditation can increase personal awareness and is good for the soul? Or, "As a man thinketh in his heart, so is he." The way we think about certain things can have a profound effect on the way we care for those things. But what happens when our thinking patterns are unhealthy due to past trauma or thought distortions?

Certain amounts of stress or anxiety are considered a normal part of life. Under these circumstances, the person can continue to function in their daily routine at a progressive rate. The stress or anxiousness may not last very long or the intensity level will decrease once the stressor is removed. Over time, if the stressor or thought process negatively intensifies and becomes overwhelming (i.e., past trauma or thought distortions), it will likely interfere with a person's daily functioning and quality of life. If these are interrupted, the probability of mental fatigue increases. For the most part, everyone wants to develop into a fully functional and operational human being who contributes to society. If we are not intentional about preserving our own mental health, then we risk mental fatigue becoming the norm for living. But fear not, as there is always hope. With psychoeducation and by incorporating a healthy self-care routine, mental fatigue can drastically decrease or even be eliminated altogether.

Mostly everyone has read about or heard someone speak about the importance of taking care of yourself through self-care. But what does taking care of yourself really mean? It can mean several different things and it could carry different meanings for different people. Some of the common trends of taking care of oneself include engaging in physical well-being, financial well-being, relational well-being, or spiritual well-being. Please note that all forms and categories of well-being are important for a balanced lifestyle. Due to increased advocacy and social awareness, the importance of persistent and consistent self-care has gained more ground over the past few years.

How can one increase their self-care for mental stability and emotional balance? In general, self-care from the mental health perspective basically means incorporating positive coping activities to help improve the peaceful balance between mood, emotions, and behavior. Self-care alludes to the idea that if mental stability and emotional balance are increased, then a person's sense of emotional and operational functioning is increased, which positively affects intrapersonal and interpersonal relationships. Self-care engagement activities can include connecting with a supportive network of people, helping others or volunteering for a worthy cause, creating a positive mindset, learning a new trade or hobby, being physically active, getting enough sleep, eating balanced meals, connecting with nature, and/or incorporating the services of a mental health professional. Additional common activities include taking a walk, aromatherapy, getting enough sunlight, listening to music, journaling, deep breathing, belly laughing, or visiting a new restaurant. There are tons of ways to incorporate self-care activities into your daily lifestyle. Focus on determining what self-care means for you and place yourself higher on your own priority list. Make the positive decision to become more aware of the things that bring you an increased sense of joy, peace, and balance.

JOIN THE MOVEMENT!
#BAUW

Becoming An Unstoppable Woman
With She Rises Studios

She Rises Studios was founded by Hanna Olivas and Adriana Luna Carlos, the mother-daughter duo, in mid-2020 as they saw a need to help empower women worldwide. They are the podcast hosts of the *She Rises Studios Podcast* and Amazon best-selling authors and motivational speakers who travel the world. Hanna and Adriana are the movement creators of #BAUW - Becoming An Unstoppable Woman: The movement has been created to universally impact women of all ages, at whatever stage of life, to overcome insecurities, and adversities, and develop an unstoppable mindset. She Rises Studios educates, celebrates, and empowers women globally.

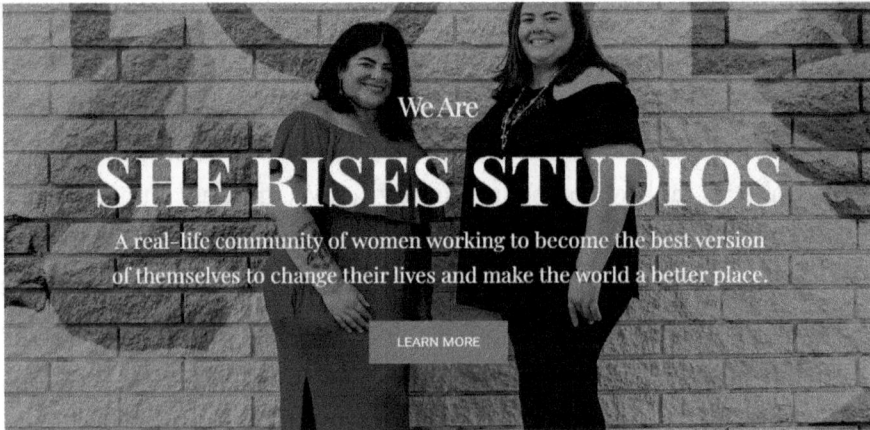

We Are
SHE RISES STUDIOS
A real-life community of women working to become the best version of themselves to change their lives and make the world a better place.

LEARN MORE

Looking to Join Us in our Next Anthology or Publish YOUR Own?

She Rises Studios Publishing offers full-service publishing, marketing, book tour, and campaign services. For more information, contact info@sherisesstudios.com

We are always looking for women who want to share their stories and expertise and feature their businesses on our podcasts, in our books, and in our magazines.

SEE WHAT WE DO

OUR PODCAST

OUR BOOKS

OUR SERVICES

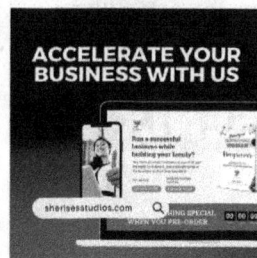

Be featured in the Becoming An Unstoppable Woman magazine, published in 13 countries and sold in all major retailers. Get the visibility you need to LEVEL UP in your business!

Have your own TV show streamed across major platforms like Roku TV, Amazon Fire Stick,

Apple TV and more!

Learn to leverage your expertise. Build your online presence and grow your audience with FENIX TV.
https://fenixtv.sherisesstudios.com/

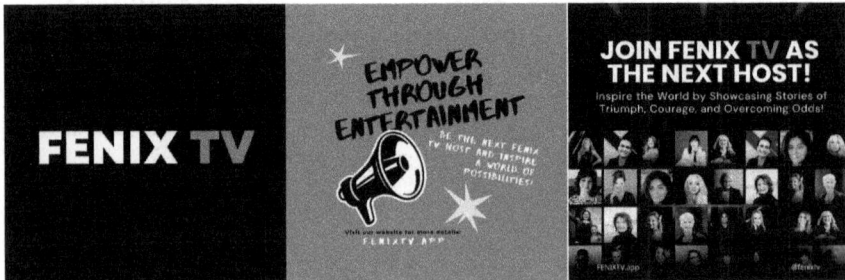

Visit www.SheRisesStudios.com to see how YOU can join the #BAUW movement and help your community to achieve the UNSTOPPABLE mindset.

Have you checked out the *She Rises Studios Podcast?*

Find us on all MAJOR platforms: Spotify, IHeartRadio, Apple Podcasts, Google Podcasts, etc.

Looking to become a sponsor or build a partnership?

Email us at info@sherisesstudios.com

SHE RISES
STUDIOS

www.ingramcontent.com/pod-product-compliance
Lightning Source LLC
Chambersburg PA
CBHW071035050426
42335CB00050B/1703